Due Diligence for Startups
A Step-by-Step Guide

Benjamin C. Lawson

DUE DILIGENCE FOR STARTUPS
A Step-by-Step Guide
© 2016 Benjamin C. Lawson

All rights reserved. Any type of reproduction, distribution, public communication or transformation of this book is only allowed under authorization of its author, excluding legal exceptions.

Please write to aflores@ieee.org to ask permission for scanning, photocopying or reproducing any fragment of this book.

© 2016 Benjamin C. Lawson
ISBN: 978-1539606826
Printed in the United States of America

To all the people who believe in a better future,
where companies serve mankind
and people enjoy their work.

To a better future besides Anna.

BENJAMIN C. LAWSON

ABOUT THE AUTHOR

Benjamin C. Lawson was born the 24th May, 1977. In 2001 mastered as a communication engineer and in 2003 as an electronics engineer.

In 2009 he got his Master in International Trade from ISEAD and in 2013, his MBA from IESE Business School, including stays in Madrid, Barcelona, Shanghai and New York.

He is an Associate at MOOS Consulting firm (www.moosconsulting.com), a consulting company focused on startups. Lawson is also the founder of three startups.

He added French and German to English and Spanish languages at the age of 14 and, in 2015, Japanese. He has been all his life in the edge of technology and he is the author of four other books related to technology and a book with a study on the meaning and translation of the Tao. He is also the author of more than 50 papers on startups and technology. Lawson is a collaborator of several institutions and associations of technology, a Member of the Advisory Board of OneTrade International LLC and Senior Member of IEEE since 2012, the biggest engineer association worldwide.

BENJAMIN C. LAWSON

CONTENTS

1. Introduction 9
2. Objectives 11
2.1. Compliance with investor's own culture 11
2.2. Know what is the value of your company 12
2.3. Highlight significant defects 12
2.4. Prepare an agreement 13
2.5. Ask for some warranties 13
3. A due diligence for every stage 15
3.1. Seed stage due diligence 17
3.2. Growth stage due diligence 18
4. Prior to start a due diligence 23
5. Step-by-step guide 27
5.1. Product portfolio 28
5.2. Market 29
5.3. Finance 32
5.4. People 37
5.5. Execution 41
5.6. Legal 47
6. Living the process 59
6.1. Timings 60
6.2. First meeting 60
6.3. Validation 61
6.4. Communication 62
6.5. Due diligence process start 63
6.6. Key personnel review 64
6.7. Term sheet 64

7.	Be prepared for many questions	65
8.	Beware the fake investors	73
8.1.	Red flag 1: no online profile	74
8.2.	Red flag 2: the man in the middle	74
8.3.	Red flag 3: ask for references	75
8.4.	Red flag 4: valuation expertise	75
8.5.	Red flag 5: "strange" term sheets	76
8.6.	Red flag 6: knowledge and contact network	76
8.7.	Red flag 7: unrealistic expectations	77
8.8.	Red flag 8: most people don't say "no"	77
8.9.	Red flag 9: gut feeling	78
8.10.	Conclusion	78

1. Introduction

A due diligence is the process typically used by an investor to verify all statements the entrepreneur team has made, to sell all or a share of the startup, are true.

Additionally, it is an important piece to guarantee the company is able to operate independently, with the appropriate processes and business model, healthy finance and a competent team.

The purpose of due diligence is to confirm or reject the assumptions others have made regarding valuation and to identify any associated risks. Poor due diligence can result in the buyer or investor being asked to pay over-the-odds for their stake, taking on unknown risks and liabilities or being unable to integrate the business, where synergy may be the primary reason for pursuing the deal.

They are all valid reasons for a buyer or investor to walk away so the entrepreneur has to guarantee an excellent work when accomplishing the due diligence process.

As a consequence, although due diligence is nothing more than a final integrity check on all aspects of the business and the team, it needs preparation, a clean execution and meet some standards in order to get the investor's trust.

When angel groups or VCs conduct due diligence of startup, they want to assure its breadth covers the entire life of the startup, beginning with its establishment and spanning into the potential future of the entity, to the extent it is reasonably predictable. The approach utilized by experienced players is typically deliberate and reflective. It is, in essence a discovery process which enables the investor to obtain an in depth understanding of the company, its technology, business model, management team, culture, processes and ultimately, whether it is worth to invest in it. Nobody enjoys the process, neither the entrepreneur nor the investor. However, for the prudent investor, it represents homework he must do to increase the potential of success with respect to a particular investment and their entire investment portfolio.

Experienced entrepreneurs recognize that they are preparing for due diligence and investor scrutiny from the very beginning of the effort, even at the concept stage. They establish a structure and processes which support the development and growth of an investible company. Taking such steps in advance of the need for outside financing is enabling in that the company is already prepared when the need arises. More importantly, it assures the startup due diligence process will validate the opportunity.

Investing in a startup equity imply a long-term business relationship, lasting an average of five years. It is very difficult for either party to get out of the deal during that period, since there is no public market for the stock, and business "divorces" normally mean bankruptcy. So it is worth your time to do a little extra work in due diligence and make the agreement a win-win deal for both sides.

In this book you will find exhaustive information not just to survive the process but to excel in maximizing your benefit in the investment agreement and also to get the funds quicker.

2. Objectives

In this section you will find the specific reasons the reasons why investors conduct due diligence in scalable startups. They can be arranged into five categories:

- Comply with investor's own culture
- Know what is the value of your company
- Highlight significant defects
- Prepare an agreement
- Ask for some warranties

Next, you can find a brief explanation on each one.

2.1. Compliance with investor's own culture

Angels and VCs invest in a particular startup opportunity when the opportunity fits their portfolios. Therefore, they establish criteria under which they invest and the due diligence process enables them to confirm whether the opportunity meets that criteria. Some criteria are openly stated and apparent, i.e. they invest in certain industries, segments, geographies or investment range. Others are less obvious and may in fact never be shared with the entrepreneur. These may include, as an example, strategic alignment with other business to which they are affiliated. This screening against criteria begins with the initial contact with the investor and continues long after the investment closes. This continued screening may, in fact, be related to the viability of additional investment in follow-up rounds.

2.2. Know what is the value of your company

There are a number of methodologies which can be utilized to determine the value of companies and assets. In the case of mature, established companies, many of the methods are analytical in nature, like DCF (Discounted Cash Flow) analysis. In the case of a scalable startup, which has very few sales and potentially modest cash flows, such valuations produce unmeaning results. In this scenario, a valuation should be based on intangible assets, like he quality and breadth of the management team, their interest in accepting coaching and their ability to execute. Although a startup does not typically have many assets, it is important all of them are measured under the investor criteria –they many differ a lot from an investor to another.

2.3. Highlight significant defects

One of the most relevant priorities of investors is the identification of defects that may be potentially fatal to the future of the company, as early as possible. Identification of material issues early in the process allows the investor and the entrepreneur to address them and potentially establish mitigation approaches. If it is not possible to mitigate the risk, the investor has the opportunity to disengage by reducing time and money spending on an opportunity that won't produce the promised results. This point is an opportunity for the entrepreneur to anticipate valuable insights about the viability of the business, as well.

However, it should be noted an opportunity may present a fatal flaw to one investor, depending on his criteria, but be attractive to another. Therefore, it should not be concluded that just because a fatal flaw exists, that startup is un-investible. It is entirely possible other angels or VCs have alternate approaches to mitigate the risk.

2.4. Prepare an agreement

As mentioned earlier, due diligence provides validation. If reasonable terms and valuations are agreed in the term sheet and the company stands up to the due diligence process well, it is possible little negotiation likely remains. Experienced angel groups and VCs are desirous of startups that stand up well to their scrutiny because it doesn't only validate their initial assumptions but it permits them to move forward other deals, using their scarce resources effectively.

2.5. Ask for some warranties

Many of the guarantees and remediation promises made as part of the closing process are standard across all deals. However, each company is different and each investor perceives risk differently. Due diligence helps identify those important items for both parties.

Entrepreneurs who have represented the facts accurately through the funding process are simply re-validating the business opportunity.

3. A due diligence for every stage

Before analyzing a startup, it is important to have in mind what are we talking about when we use the word startup. According to Wikipedia, a startup company is "an entrepreneurial venture which is typically a newly emerged, fast-growing business that aims to meet a marketplace need by developing or offering an innovative product, process or service. A startup is usually a company such as a small business, a partnership or an organization designed to rapidly develop scalable business model".

Although this is the most widespread meaning when referring to a startup, an entrepreneurial venture is technically called a startup during a shorter period of time, as shown in Fig. 1, that is, after having experienced the first successes in terms of significant sales –so called growth stage– and just before handing over the maturity stage, i.e. going public.

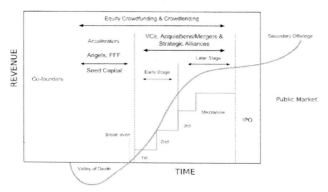

Fig. 1. Typical financing cycles in a startup

However, we are covering all the stages shown in Fig. 2 in terms of performing a due diligence on a startup, from seed capital to latter venture capital (VC) investments.

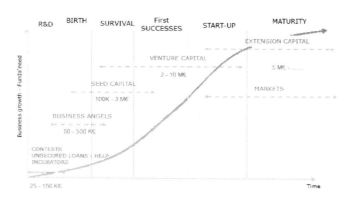

Fig. 2. Typical financing ranges for each stage

3.1. Seed stage due diligence

This is most relevant for angels and early-stage VCs. At this stage the company would at most be a few founders and a prototype. The most important things for an investor at this stage to do are as follows:

- Jobs to be done (JTBD): is there a real market need? Speak to potential customers.

- Team capability: does the team have necessary skill sets to execute and the temperament to sail through the ups and downs? Meet up with team members individually and do reference checks on key founders.

- Competitive landscape: prepare a summary of local and global players in the same or similar area and collect as much information as possible.

- Exit potential: prepare a list of potential acquirers and document why they would acquire a company like this.

- Founder's pre-nuptial: ask founders to document the terms of their co-working arrangements. Verbal agreements or inappropriate drafting of these arrangements can cause lot of disturbance for the company. If possible, also need to get founders to sign a non-disclosure and non-compete in case of a break-up.

- Employee contracts: ask for employment, non-disclosure and non-compete agreements duly signed by all part-time as well as full-time employees. If there are employees abroad, look out for their legal employment status.

- Pre-existing liabilities: ask founders to disclose all pre-existing liabilities including options granted or notes issued to third parties. Get them to sign an undertaking.

- Licensing agreements: if the entire technology or a part of that technology is licensed from an external party, the terms and conditions of usage of technology should be properly documented.
- Record keeping: select some transactions from the financials –if any available– and look for supporting documents.
- Co-investors: meet up and get comfortable with key co-investors, particularly those who are close to founders.

3.2. Growth stage due diligence

This is a stage when there is lesser ambiguity than seed stage. The company would likely have more data points and records to ensure a more detailed due diligence. This is a stage where involving a CPA (Certified Public Accountant) and a lawyer makes sense. But it is still not possible to outsource all of the required due diligence, at least if you don't have a professional consulting firm specialized in due diligences for startups. The reason is that lawyers and CPAs are not usually very familiar with technology startups and partly because there are areas that they won't have a clue.

At this stage, the most important items to watch for are the following.

3.2.1. Value proposition

- Look out for the "unfair advantage" and verify that by

speaking to at least one or two industry professionals. It can be the technology, business model or a combination of both.

- Obtain a competitor landscape from the founders and verify that independently. Big red flag if founders have missed out on some prominent ones.
- Get details of strategic alliances, joint ventures or other partnerships. Check if any of that might become a roadblock in future exit plans.
- If the company has multiple products, obtain features and pricing details for the entire product range.
- Request for details of "use of capital" and ensure that it makes overall sense.

3.2.2. Investment history

- Obtain a capital structure table (cap table) and verify that with data independently obtained from government agencies (like ACRA in Singapore or ROC extracts in India) or independent data providers. Ensure all convertible notes, stock options, warrants, etc. are fully disclosed to calculate fully diluted outstanding shareholding pattern of the company.
- Ask for a copy of previous shareholders and subscription agreements. Go through previous investors rights and options to participate in the current round.
- Meet up with at least all the investor representatives on the board of directors. It is important to establish that the future board is going to be functional.

3.2.3. Legal and secretarial

- Get a copy of memoranda and articles of association to ensure that they are up to date and reflect all the changes made during the previous investment rounds.
- Obtain minutes of all previous board and shareholders meetings.
- Ask founders to provide details of all existing, previous and threatened legal disputes, litigation, arbitration or judgements. A declaration or undertaking from the founders that information provided is complete to the best of their knowledge is also desirable.
- Ask for details of all patent, trademark, copyright applications, in progress or granted.
- Go through all licensing and other agreements.

3.2.4. Financial performance and projections

- Get a copy of latest board approved budget, management accounts and audited financials, if available. Compare revenue and expenses between budget and actual accounts to identify and explore deviations. This can also be used to analyze future projections.
- Review gross margins and net margins for each product line and assess if direct expenses have been pushed below the line as overheads.
- Analyze working capital items: debtors, creditors and inventory. Ageing list can be very helpful.
- Ensure that amounts due to technology and other service providers are accrued and recorded in

accordance with agreements as liability even though they are not paid out.

- Obtain details of bank mandates and signatory limits.
- Obtain copy of bank statements for all the accounts held in company's name. Match bank balances with the latest audited and unaudited financials provided.
- Ensure that the company has filed all its tax and annual returns with relevant authorities. Get copies of tax assessment notices.
- Carefully look for related party transactions and ensure that they were conducted at arm length.
- Go through the list of fixed assets and verify material items. If there are huge intangible assets capitalized in the balance sheet, make sure that they are valued realistically.

3.2.5. Human resources

- Get a copy of company's organizational chart and list of employees with their roles.
- Verify employment contracts, non-disclosure and non-compete agreements, where applicable.
- Look for historical attrition rates to identify unusually high staff turnover.
- Ensure that all the employees have the right to work in the country they are based in. Also, verify that the company has been promptly paying the employer's contributions in accordance with local laws.

3.2.6. Technical

Technical aspects depend a lot on the sector whether it is software, hardware, biotech, clean-tech, etc. although there are some common themes:

- Capability of the technology: to ensure it does what it promises, schedule a demo. Prepare a walk-through of various use cases. For software, go through the functionality from both front and admin ends and document screen shots. For biotech, look for data coming out of independent trials.

- Stability and scalability: this is relevant primarily for software startups where architecture, algorithms and databases need to be assessed for stability and scalability. Obtain a list of infrastructure monitoring tools used by the company. Get a description of redundancies built into the hosting platform and hardware.

- Usage data: obtain monthly traffic reports like site visitors, unique visitors, registered users, returning users, etc.

- Third party tools: obtain a list of third party tools and content utilized by or embedded within company products. Ensure that licenses are in place.

- Development roadmap: review company plans and "use of capital sheet" to assess if significant pivot in product direction are anticipated in coming years.

- Ownership: evaluate academic affiliations of the founders and CTO to assess competing claims on the technology. If the technology is licensed from a research institute, assess the impact in an exit scenario.

4. Prior to start a due diligence

Experienced entrepreneurs keep in mind they will require investment in their companies sooner or later. As a result, they conduct a "due-diligence-ready" management style into their companies, that is, considering certain information, structure or relationships are managed in a way a due diligence exercise in the future will be the easier as possible.

However, once the due diligence process comes across, it is important to take some advice:

- **Appoint one of the founders as the leader** of the process. He will coordinate the advisors and work the personal relations with potential investors. This reduces the impact on current business and sales, because due diligence implies intense and extenuating work, demanding a lot of attention and time.

- Once you have identified the **internal champion** among the investor's team, that is, the one interested in closing the deal and with enough power to persuade others in his organization, the appointed leader in your company should build the stronger personal relationship possible with him and give him the tools to sell the deal internally. Best practices are: sharing good news, data and new agreements with him, explaining the issues and the way they can be overcome in order he can minimize the impact on the other side, etc.

- Manage the **information stream** appropriately, releasing the data accordingly to the message you want to transmit, presenting the positive face of the numbers (sales, users, etc.) and not just cold and bold reports. Don't give all the good news at a time and do the same with bad news. Please keep in mind there are people with their own feelings on the other side, even despite they try to show themselves as cold calculators.

- **Always tell the truth.** A lie can destroy trust among the parties and that will mean the end of the deal. You should show that you can manage uncertainty as an entrepreneur, so never invent. Nobody expects everything is perfect but that you do have a plan to face things that are going wrong.

- **Stick to your numbers** as much as possible. Entrepreneurs are usually ugly giving projections. Anyway, the more accurate your forecast is the stronger your ability to execute will be considered. Investors will trust your valuation and growth plan better if you demonstrate you don't deviate too much from your own expectations.

- For technology-driven startups looking to attract a buyer or additional investment, ensuring the **intellectual property portfolio is "due diligence ready"** is essential for sale or investment to progress easily. A top tip is to make sure the inventors are correctly identified and that the chain of title is clear and well-documented. Make sure that all necessary assignments are correctly executed (and registered, where appropriate) and save yourself time further on in the due diligence process by uploading all documents to your central data room.

- Due diligence is **not a binding document**. It means far from you being able to ask to remove additional warranties in the contract because the investor had the chance to analyze all the details of your company, it can be used by the investor to reduce the valuation of the company, ask for additional warranties, etc.

- Keep in mind the due diligence objective is to share enough information so the investor can take a positive decision to invest in your company but **not to replicate your business** if the deal is not closed. Never forget that an investor can be a competitor in some circumstances.

BENJAMIN C. LAWSON

5. Step-by-step guide

Every VC or angel investor is different and due diligence checklists have to be provided tactfully based on the specific investor.

However, here you can find a standard list of company information that most institutional investors will look for during the due diligence process. It is an extensive list but not exhaustive and all applicable, depending on the company stage or maturity and nature. Founders and management team should consider preparing and organizing themselves with the below to make the process as smooth as possible.

Sometimes it is better to hire an expert to lead all the due diligence process in order to free up the investor team's valuable time. By the way, this is what I do for my customers in MOOS Consulting ;)

Anyway, let's see the six main parts of a due diligence and a list of information typically requested for each one:

- Product due diligence
- Market due diligence
- Finance due diligence
- People due diligence
- Execution due diligence
- Legal due diligence

5.1. Product portfolio

When speaking of products, it is important to know not just the portfolio but the future roadmap, the value proposition to customers and quality aspects required to guarantee sustainable products along time.

In this section, due diligence will cover most of the following items.

5.1.1. Existing and former products

- Provide detailed product and services documentation that includes feature descriptions, architecture and design, technical performance specifications and other relevant details. Give specific attention to demonstrated capability of the products and solutions where applicable. Specially describe the characteristics of the largest product deployment, as a good example.

- List all current products and services, explain how long they have been available and what the evolution of features and timeline has been.

- List all products that have been de-emphasized or discontinued in the past –if any– and explain the reasons for that decision. Indicate whether the former product has been replaced by a newer product.

- Provide a table with strengths and weaknesses for each product, from technology and competitive viewpoints, and indicate the plan and timeline to address shortcomings where appropriate.

- List all 3rd party, intellectual property (IP) rights and open source dependencies involved to produce each product or service, where applicable.

5.1.2. Product quality

- List all product CE compliance status and other regulatory agencies that are appropriate.
- Provide the previous 12 months of product defect and trouble history with dates. Present a chart if needed to clarify the picture of how the company is doing in terms of quality.

5.1.3. Product and service roadmap

- Provide current product development roadmap that also identifies in-process versus future efforts.
- Provide a product pipeline: a view of current development status versus planned status, delayed efforts, an explanation and countermeasures.

5.2. Market

Entrepreneur knowledge about the market is very important for investors. They are usually looking for people with a profound knowledge of the key drivers in the market they are operating, a strong sense of how money can be invested to beat competition and a clear view of the abilities and limitations of their company.

5.2.1. Competing scenario

In this part it is important you perform a Porter analysis of the company, which consists of identifying the five competing forces for the products and services the company offers, as shown in Fig. 3.

Fig. 3. Five forces in Porter's model

5.2.2. Competing strategy

Once the playground is clear, the next step is to set how the company is going to perform, in what direction, how it will thrive among issues and challenges that will appear, and how it will manage implementation, opportunities, risks, new business and productivity models at a high-level perspective.

- List all alliance partners and strategic partners, key stakeholders that will help the company gain market share among competitors.
- State competing strategy. A good way to represent competing strategy is to do a SWOT analysis, as shown in Fig. 4.

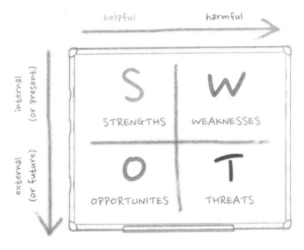

Fig. 4. SWOT Analysis structure

5.2.3. Customers

- State your base customers in terms of number and revenue. Avoid providing customer names or data, as you have to keep in mind there is no closed deal at this point of negotiation.
- Add beta customers, trial subscriptions, newsletter lists and everything that may be converted into a customer

in the future, never providing names or personal details.

- Provide customer dynamics as well, like customer conversion rates, time a customer usually takes from being a prospect in a trial or newsletter until he signs off a contract, etc.

5.2.4. Competition

- List all competitors with their strengths and weaknesses against the company.
- Avoid any statement regarding no competitors are in place. There is no such thing. There are always competitors. It may not be directly in what you are doing, but having the understanding and knowledge of the entire landscape and being able to articulate it and explain how you are different is impressive.
- Never say you are doing something that has never been done. It is not true. People have definitely tried doing it before but were not successful. Research them and learn from their mistakes. Then present the investor the decisions the previous founders had taken and how your company is differentiating.

5.3. Finance

Finance is critical for any funding venture and especially for startups, because it is the quantitative part that allows the investor to imagine a future scenario, some years after the investment is made.

Finance due diligence is probably the most intense part in terms of time effort. It is about guaranteeing your company is up to date within taxes and government requirements and it is also about the expectations on the company for the future, in terms of profit and return on investment.

5.3.1. Financial basics

- Capital structure: outstanding shares, line of credits, bank debts, stockholders details, options, warrants, rights, dilutive securities details, additional liabilities.
- Income statements, P&L, balance sheet, cash flow, account receivables, management financial briefings, sales numbers, planned vs actual for the last three years.
- Financial projections: quarterly projections for 3-5 years, growth prospects, capital expenditures, depreciation and working capital.
- Taxes, net losses, revenue recognition, implied valuations for earlier rounds, business traction predictability, risks, industry pricing policies and any additional financing.

5.3.2. Financial statements

- Audited financial statements and management letters issued by auditors in respect of the audits, if any.
- Copy of the most recent business plan and budget covering the last three years.
- Analysis of operating, general and administration expenses, in absolute value and as a percentage of revenues by significant category for the last three years and the current YTD period.

- Monthly financial reporting packages distributed to senior management.
- Sales by country in the last year.

5.3.3. Related party transactions

- Summary of sales or purchases, sales, service arrangements to or from related parties, including principal terms and whether at arm length, including inter-company receivables and payable balances. Include description of services provided by or to related parties.

5.3.4. Balance sheet

For the last three years and the current YTD period, provide the following:

- Cash
    - Bank reconciliations, including bank statements for the current YTD period and previous three year-end periods.
    - A listing of any restrictions on cash.
    - Accounts receivable.
    - Accounts receivable aging analysis and trends for the last three years and the most recent available month.
    - History of allowance for doubtful accounts balance, bad debt expense and write-offs, and reserves for sales returns, discounts, rebates, refunds, and credit memos in the last three years and the current available month.
- Inventory

- Inventory balances by location, major product group and type: raw materials, work in process and finished goods.
- Summary of inventory write-offs and basis used to develop obsolete and slow-moving inventory reserves, including any history of sales and write-offs of obsolete and overstock inventory.

- Manufacturing and purchasing
  - Summary of locations and descriptions of subcontracted manufacturing facilities.
  - List of top 10 significant suppliers by purchasing amount and detail of purchased supplies from each.
  - List of any production or sales made under license or royalty agreements.

- Prepaid expenses and other assets: schedule of prepaid expenses and other long and short-term assets, considering goodwill, intangibles and amortization criteria, including assessment of potential recovery.

- Property and equipment
  - Schedule of fixed assets, including date acquired, original cost, accumulated depreciation, net book value and recent appraised value.
  - List of historical, current and planned for the next 3 years capital expenditures, separated by major category (e.g. machinery, MIS, buildings etc.).

- Accounts payable and accrued liabilities
  - Accounts payable, aging schedule and significant accrued expense accounts for the last three

years and the most recent available month.

- o Details of customer deposits and any deferred revenues by type and customer for the last three years and the current YTD period.
- o Warranty expense and sales returns history (expense and reserves) for the last three years and a description of how the warranty and sales returns reserves were developed.

- Contingencies and litigation: summary of pending, threatened or asserted litigation claims and any legal accruals, including contingent liabilities, product liability claims and outstanding supplier claims.
- Agreements: joint venture, partnership or trust agreements with respect to which the company is a party.

5.3.5. Proprietary technology

- Detailed list of all patents, applications, trademarks and copyrights. It is important to list not just the issued IP and patents but also those that are pending.
- List of all previous and current patent infringement situations and legal issues related to IP, outbound and inbound.
- List of all contractors and their contractual rights to IP ownership.
- List of geographical patent protection issues.
- All trademarks and proof of registration along with any history of infringement disputes or actions.

5.3.6. Facilities

- Property, if any.
- Copy of fully executed leases and all amendments.
- Summary of any lease expirations or options occurring in the next 12 months and the current status and work effort toward these, e.g. have notices been issued or renewals in negotiation.
- Description and estimated cost for any in-progress or deferred capital improvements.

5.4. People

In a startup, it is important to analyze the entrepreneur in first place and then the rest of his team, because the company has much to do with its founder and its future may depend on how well he can evolve during the different maturity stages that will occur in the next years after the investment venture.

5.4.1. The entrepreneur

- Character: is he...
    - a street-smart or a book-smart founder
    - a risk taker or a highly planned person
    - aiming his company for a short-term or a long-term exit
    - an aggressive or an easy-going entrepreneur
    - raised from an earlier hard fall or not

- passionate for the startup or not
- Experience with VCs or angels:
  - How does he perceive the valuation of the startup by the VC
  - What role is he expecting from the VC: just an investor or someone for mentoring and acceleration help.
  - Has there been previous investment rounds
- Personal investment: has the founder invested his personal money and time?

5.4.2. The executive team

In a typical startup, the executive team –and probably the whole team- has to be less than 10 people. If it is a higher figure, the investor will be worried or may even quit the process.

- Provide an organization chart, projected headcount, compensation arrangement, incentive stock plans, employee relations, benefit plans.
- Is there a plan for the founder CEO succession issue?
- List copies of executive employment agreements, severance agreement and change in control agreement.
- Executive-only health, disability and perquisite benefits with a list of participants.
- Deferred compensation summary plan document with a list of participants and amount deferred by each participant.

5.4.3. Organization

- Organizational charts for each department and function.
- Employee handbook and human resource policies, as well as new hire orientation documents.
- List of all locations and number of employees, if more than one.

5.4.4. Workforce

- List of all employees which includes ID number, name, job title, manager, annual base salary, annual bonus percentage, job function, department, date of hire, location, country, currency, union/non-union, FLSA status, date of birth, prior year W-2, full time/part-time status, etc.
- List of all leased employees or independent contractors which includes ID number, name, job title, manager, annual base salary, annual bonus percentage, job function, department, date of hire, date assignment to complete, location, country, currency, name of agency.

5.4.5. Compensation

- Copy of salary structures, compensation philosophy and methodology.
- Policy and practice on general wage or salary increases and administration of program, if any.
- Special retention plans; list of participants with details of payouts.

5.4.6. Equity programs

- Summary plan document for stock option programs, including non-qualified stock options, incentive stock options, restricted stock options, Employee Stock Ownership Plan (ESOP) and Employee Stock Purchase Plan (ESSP).
- List of employees who have received stock options or RSUs which includes name, department, job title, strike price, stock amount, stock value, vesting date, country.
- List of participants in the ESOP program.

5.4.7. Incentive compensation

- Incentive compensation plans and list of participants.
- 3-year payout history and projected pay out.

5.4.8. Employee benefits

- Summary of benefit plans, domestic and international.
- Copy of contracts/agreement with Third Party Administrators (TPAs), domestic and international.
- List of participants in each benefit, including monthly employee contribution for each benefit and company paid portion of benefits.

5.4.9. Retirement plans

- Defined benefit pension plan if appropriate, active or frozen.

- Defined contribution plan: copy of the non-discrimination testing results, including the available investment options.
- Supplemental retirement benefits summary plan document and list of participants, if any.
- Retiree medical obligations, actuarial evaluation, whether active or frozen.

5.4.10. Severance program

- Plan document, written policy or agreement.
- Description of severance payments over the last 2 years.
- Forms 5500 and schedules for last 3 years.

5.4.11. Immigration and work status

- List of all expats, immigrants and non-resident aliens by country in which they are working and their visa status.
- Any actual or threatened I-9 audit or information request by the government.

5.5. Execution

Execution is part of sales, part of service delivery and part of general company operations. It means the ability of the executive team to run the company in a profitable way.

The investor will be highly interested in the

company current customers as well as continuity of customers. As a result, there is a strong emphasis on customer track record, customer agreements for the coming years and termination clauses for customer contracts.

In terms of service delivery, the investor will be focused on how standardized the operating processes are in the company, in order to ease future scaling.

5.5.1. Sales

- Detailed sales organizational views by resources, territories and accounts.
- Orders and sales by customer in each of last 3 years.
- Orders and sales by product in each of last 3 years.
- Orders and sales by geographical region in each of last 3 years.
- Orders and sales by vertical industry segment in each of last 3 years.
- Orders and sales in each of last 3 years by incumbent customers versus new customers.
- Orders and sales in each of last 3 years for existing products versus new products.
- Top 20 customers (by sales in $) in each of the past 3 years, indicating per year sales and what products and services composed the total purchasing amount.
- Most current sales operations report, inclusive of activities, forecasts and performance metrics.
- Most current sales funnel and composition, today and a year ago by product, region and industry segment.

- Past 12 month win/loss analysis by region, product and customer.
- Discounting trend over past 3 years.
- Currently pending POs.
- Currently open bids.
- Top 10 forecasted opportunities for next 12 months.
- Detailed explanation of sales compensation plan.

5.5.2. Outbound marketing and corporate communication

- Outbound marketing budget and expenditures for past 3 years.
- Most current marketing operations report, inclusive of activities, forecasts and performance metrics.

5.5.3. Revenue and customer information

- Orders, sales (in both $ & units) and gross margin by major product group, customer type and by geographic region for the last three years and the current YTD period.
- Description of non-recurring revenue (including large one-time orders), non-product revenue (royalty, licensing, trademark or patent revenues), and unusual and extraordinary items for the last three years and the current YTD period.
- Schedule showing firm order backlog, by product line as of the most current date and as of the comparable date in the preceding year (include estimated gross margin and expected sales timing of orders in

backlog).

- Top 10 customers ranked by sales for each of the last three years and current YTD period.
- Listing of significant new customers and lost customers in the last three years.

5.5.4. General operational processes

- Provide delivery metrics, standard lead-times and yields by product model.
- List of facilities, leased or owned, addresses, and square footage used for manufacturing, if any.
- Expected changes in facilities requirements in the next 2 to 3 years.
- List major equipment expense required for the production and test processes, indicating leasing condition or owned, age, estimated annual down time and expected 2-3 year annual capital budget and estimated annual maintenance.

5.5.5. Manufacturing and supply chain system

- Provide details on manufacturing and finance systems (ERP), if any.
- Describe if there is any implementation of material planning and control process (MRP, Buy to Forecast, JIT, Supplier Managed Inv., Kanban, etc.).
- Provide inventory details:

    o Last 12 months ending inventory value, by site and product.

- Last 12 months ending inventory turns metric.
- Last 12 months of inventory adjustments (cost management, loss, scrap, etc.).
- Any inventory held in consignment or consigned to others.

- Provide supply chain details: top 10 suppliers, their address and the annual direct material spends with each.

5.5.6. Quality and compliance

- List all quality compliance certifications (ISO, TL)
- Provide field return metrics by product model
- List all product certifications (CE, UL, FCC, ect.) and compliances (NEBS, RoHS, ect.) by product model
- Provide details of hazardous waste disposal, emissions or required environmental permits and status
- Provide details of safety programs such as MSDS document control, OSHA audits and Workman's Compensation claims
- Provide export codes (ECCN, HTS) and any required export licenses by product model
- List all products that have encryption and/or decryption capabilities
- List all countries shipped to by product model

5.5.7. Services delivery and support

- Detailed service, support and operation organizational (SSO) views by resources, territories and accounts.

- Most current SSO operations report, inclusive of activities, forecasts and performance metrics.
- Define the warranty coverage and period plans.
- Provide the last three customer satisfaction surveys or equivalent.
- Provide a customer list with the number of trouble tickets each has had in each of the prior three years and what the current state is.

5.5.8. Customer journey

This is an important part in a startup, as it represents what a customer will experience when interacting with the company and how it will respond to each request, purchase, claim, etc.

- Describe how fast the company iterates to meet the customer needs on time. That is the speed of development and it is related to how fast a change in a product or service can be accomplished.
- Document how the company can deliver a product at the scale needed. This is related to reliability in terms of what can happen if a customer orders a higher amount of product or service than usual.
- List any standardized processes for interacting with customers and describe them.
- Describe what happens when customers demand product or services out of standards.

5.6. Legal

Legal aspects are not usually the best part for a startup. The founders typically relay on some professionals this part and, frequently, there are some misunderstandings due to the use to standard templates and terms for signing contracts, defining the company structure and other aspects where, at the end, are probably the most relevant ones in a startup, given the unique and new business models it usually follow.

All papers and documents that may have legal implications or that are part of legal or administrative authorities requirements are under the scope of the legal due diligence.

A list of the expected documents to be requested by an investor is shown in this section, in eight categories.

5.6.1. Basic company documents and history

- Provide the full list of shareholders. It is important in a first round of investment ("A" round) the number of them is less than 10.

- All signed resolutions, including written consents, of or reports prepared for the board of directors or any comparable governing body of the company, as applicable, and any of their respective committees, including copies of any written notices or waivers thereof.

- Minutes of all meetings and all signed resolutions (including written consents) of the shareholders, members or partners of the company, as applicable, including copies of any written notices or waivers thereof.

- For the past three years, all news or press releases issued by or with respect to the company.

- A list of all domestic and foreign jurisdictions in which the company maintains an office, owns or leases property, where employees are located, is otherwise qualified to do business as a foreign entity, or is required to be qualified to do business as a foreign entity.

- A list of current directors and officers of the company (including name, age, position and length of service), together with current salaries and bonuses.

- Internal operational manuals and organization charts.

- A summary of business and personal relationships and affiliations among directors, officers, shareholders, creditors, customers, suppliers and other business affiliates.

- All reports and any other communications to stockholders.

5.6.2. Securities

- A list of the current stockholders of the company.

- Stock books and ledgers of the company.

- A schedule of outstanding options, warrants or any other contracts, commitments, agreements or promises, oral or written, with respect to the issuance, subscription, purchase, sale or transfer of any securities of the company, including grantee, dates of issuance, exercise price, vesting term and duration where applicable.

- A list of authorized, issued and outstanding

securities of the company, by type of security and converted basis, including stockholder names and tax identification numbers, date of issuance, consideration received, number of vested and unvested shares and vesting schedules. Indicate if vesting of anyone of them will impact on accelerating a merger or changing the control of the company.

- Copies of all other convertible securities of the company.

- Details of any charges or other encumbrances or claims relating to any securities of the company.

- Voting agreements, voting trusts, redemption agreements, stockholder agreements, registration rights agreements, restrictive agreements, stock purchase and repurchase agreements, stock restriction agreements and other similar agreements, contracts or commitments to which the company or any of its directors, officers or stockholders is a party.

- Agreements for the purchase of securities from the company and any private placement memoranda or offering circulars.

- Other contracts or agreements relating to the company securities, including broker, dealer or selling agent agreements.

5.6.3. Insiders

- Details of board and management perquisites and similar arrangements.

- Documents pertaining to any receivables from or payables to any director, officer, partner, stockholder or affiliate of the company.

- All agreements and guaranties between the company and any current or former officers, directors, stockholders and partners, with a description of them.

- Details of any bankruptcy or insolvency of any of the shareholders or directors of the company and details of any insolvency of a company or other entity of which any of the directors was a director, officer or shareholder.

5.6.4. Documents related to indebtedness

- Documents and agreements evidencing borrowings, whether secured or unsecured, and other long-term or short-term indebtedness, including indentures, credit or loan agreements, debentures, commitment letters, letters of credit, etc, relating to any outstanding or available long-term or short-term debt, including amendments and any related instruments granting security interests.

- Debt schedule, identifying all short-term and long-term debt and capital lease obligations with principal amounts, interest rates, balance outstanding and maturity dates.

- Documents and agreements evidencing other material financing arrangements, installment purchases, etc.

- All documents relating to financings with investors, including any accredited investor questionnaires, if applicable.

- List and copies of all financing statements currently in effect.

- Schedule of liens and encumbrances against any of the

company assets or stock, whether or not of public record.

- Documents and agreements evidencing surety and other bond arrangements.
- List and documentation of all loans made by the company, including loans to officers, directors and employees.
- Correspondence with company lenders, regarding any default or alleged default.

5.6.5. Contracts and commitments

- All agreements with customers currently in effect or under consideration and a schedule of major customers for each product line, giving annual dollar amounts sold.
- All agreements with distributors or sales representatives regarding the sale of the products or services.
- All agreements with dealers, suppliers and service providers involving more than $25,000; all reseller (including VARs, OEMs, dealers, sales representatives, etc.), retail distribution (including service and support contracts, marketing agreements, etc.), advertising, and related agreements involving more than $25,000; and schedule of major suppliers (indicate if any are sole source contracts), giving annual dollar amounts purchased.
- All agreements entered into out of the ordinary course of business, including consulting, development, capital commitments, technology sharing, cooperation, joint research and joint venture agreements.

- All contracts, arrangements, plans, and understandings to which any director, officer, shareholder, partner or other affiliate of the company, on the one hand, and the company, on the other hand, are parties, including loans and guaranties.

- All employment contracts with management and other employees; deferred compensation agreements, severance agreements, settlement agreements, consulting agreements or any other agreements with any independent contractor or consultant (including information as to whether the consultant was previously an employee), and similar agreements; all non-competition agreements, non-solicitation agreements, non-piracy agreements, non-disclosure agreements, agreements containing restrictive covenants and similar agreements addressing the company rights to inventions or other intellectual property; all indemnification agreements with employees, former employees or consultants and similar agreements; all employee or supervisor handbooks or manuals and similar agreements; and all conflicts of interest or ethics codes or policies and similar materials.

- Copies of all non-competition agreements, non-solicitation agreements, non-piracy agreements, secrecy agreements, non-disclosure agreements and standstill agreements to which the company is a party.

- Copies of all operating agreements involving more than $25,000, including without limitation, agreements to package, store, deliver or dispose of inventory.

- Copies of all agreements involving more than $25,000 obligating the company to carry on or facilitate business on behalf of another party or, conversely, obligating another party to carry on or facilitate business on behalf of the company.

- Copies of all services agreements involving more than $25,000 (e.g., property maintenance, advertising, lodging, transportation, catering, landscaping, etc.).

- Standard forms of customer agreements, distributor agreements, sales representative agreements, employment agreements, licensing agreements, leases, reseller agreements, dealer agreements, purchase orders, and sales orders used in connection with purchases, licensing, sales and leases.

- All government contracts, samples of subcontracting forms, affirmative action plans and supporting data.

- All guarantees of, and all indemnifications relating to, the company obligations and all guarantees or indemnifications by the company, any predecessor entity or its officers, directors or partners of the obligations of any other person or entity.

- Description and copy of any bargaining agreements or any other agreements involving a union at the company and the date when any such agreement is open for renegotiation; description of labor unrest situations; all pending or threatened labor strikes or other labor trouble experienced by company; description of any current or expected attempts to unionize; description of labor relationships, turnover experience and bargaining history; and grievance files.

- List of all current consultants and independent contractors of the company (including name, age, position and length of service), together with current compensation.

- All other material contracts not otherwise described herein with a remaining term in excess of one year or involving amounts in excess of $25,000 or rights or obligations of equivalent value.

5.6.6. Litigation and claims

- Summaries of all litigation and dispute resolution; memoranda of all outstanding litigation and disputes and of all litigation or disputes settled or otherwise terminated, containing the following information: parties, venue, nature of proceeding, date commenced, and amount of damages or other relief sought; and access to all pleadings on file regarding such litigation and relevant insurance coverage.

- Summary of nature and amount of all unrecorded and contingent liabilities (including threatened claims and causes of action), warranty experience, products liability exposure, environmental contamination, employee problems, and material disputes with third parties; and copies of all relevant correspondence.

- Summaries and memoranda relating to any governmental or administrative investigations, proceedings or arbitrations, whether pending, threatened or concluded, to which the company is or was subject; and access to all relevant documentation regarding such investigations, proceedings and arbitrations.

- All consent decrees, court and administrative judgments and orders, settlements, injunctions, etc., requiring or prohibiting future activities of the company.

- All opinions by counsel as to any pending litigation against the company, including letters to auditors.

- Copies of any documents related to any internal investigation or review by the company, including without limitation related to any actual or alleged misconduct by an employee, consultant, sales representative, distributor or other representative of the company, regardless of whether such investigation or review resulted in a finding of wrongdoing.

- Listing of all charges or claims filed against the company with any administrative agency, including, without limitation, the Department of Labor, the Equal Employment Opportunity Commission, Occupational Safety and Health Administration, Social Security Administration, Unemployment Commission, Office of Federal Contract Compliance Programs or any state or local counterparts and any documents related to such charges or claims.

5.6.7. Tangible properties

- Listing of all real estate owned, leased, subleased, or used. State whether the property is owned or leased (whether as lessor or lessee) and list the entity or individual which holds the title or lease and describe the property, liens thereon, structures, lease provisions, use and location.

- Copies of all deeds, leases, mortgages, sales contracts, surveys, sublease contracts, appraisals, environmental studies, and with respect to leased properties, all notices of default under such leases and estoppel letters executed by the Company.

- Zoning information and records relating to zoning violations, approvals, special exceptions, and nonconforming uses.

- All existing real property interests, including without limitation rights of first refusal, etc., relating to any property listed above.

- Copy of all leases, licenses and similar agreements relating to real property, with all schedules and amendments thereto.

- All title and appraisal reports and title insurance policies with respect to any properties or assets of the Company.

- Copies of all leases to moveable property and personal property.

- Copies of all asset lists, including a list of all assets not located on real property owned or leased by the Company.

5.6.8. Intangible properties

- Schedule of all foreign and domestic trademarks, service marks, logos, corporate names, trade names, and all applications to register (including intent-to-use applications), registrations, oppositions, cancellations or other proceedings challenging the ownership or validity of the marks used by the company.

- Schedule of all foreign and domestic patents, patent applications, inventions disclosures, and reexaminations, reissues, oppositions or other proceedings challenging the ownership or validity in connection therewith.

- Schedule of all registered copyrights and applications for copyright registration, material unregistered copyrights (including rights in software and databases) and all proceedings challenging ownership or validity in connection therewith.

- Schedule showing the relationship of each identified patent right to the company products and services (e.g., which company products are covered by which company patents)

- All agreements involving the transfer or right to use intellectual property rights to which the company is a party, whether as licensor, sub-licensor, licensee or sub-licensee, including research, product development, software (including open source code), distribution or marketing.

- Company written policy and procedures for selecting, clearing, using and protecting trademarks; for selecting patent disclosures for patent protection; for preparing and prosecuting patent applications; enforcing patent rights and avoiding infringement of the rights of others; and protecting copyrighted materials.

- Confidentiality and non-disclosure agreements with employees and with any other persons, such as actual or potential consultants, developers, vendors or customers, with respect to proprietary information.

- Company written policy and procedures for protecting company confidential and trade secret information.

- Company written policy and procedures for the use of open-source software and a listing of all open source licenses under which open source code is used or incorporated in company software.

- Copies of all notices and correspondence relating to allegations of infringement or misappropriation of third-party intellectual property rights by the Company and the company intellectual property rights by third parties.

6. Living the process

Due diligence is a very important milestone in the life of a startup, for two reasons mainly:

- It is a thorough analysis of the "as is" state of the company, thus it is a valuable occasion to get the most accurate picture of how is it doing and how is it to be in the future.

- It will be the most important asset the company will have to discuss and negotiate with investors the best terms and conditions for the future and health of the company.

Some entrepreneurs do very little to prepare for due diligence, assuming all the talking has already been done and the business plan and results to date tell everything one needs to know. On the other hand, others tend to schedule exhaustive meetings and training sessions for the team, including showcase customers, to make sure everyone paints a consistent picture when facing the investors. One way or another, it is important to know what are the stages of the process and what outcomes one should expect from each one.

Every VC or business angel is different and due diligence answers need to be provided tactfully based on the investor's earlier investment track record. In this chapter you will understand what the investor will probably expect from an entrepreneur along the process, to go the smoothest and quickest possible until the end.

6.1. Timings

Founders need to remember meetings prior to due diligence have been primarily off site, with staged demos and managed personally by the CEO or a small team. Due diligence always involves on-site visits, informal discussions with any or all members of the team, vendors, good and bad customers.

Based on the size of the investment and the runway available, the due diligence process can take several weeks or even a couple of months to complete. In any case, before the process begins, you should be doing your own *reverse* due diligence on the investor. In chapter 8 you will find some advice.

Last but not least, if there are conflicts within the team, differing views of the strategy or evidence of missing processes and tools, the investment process will likely be terminated. That is the reason why you should plan resources, timings and interactions in advance.

6.2. First meeting

The goal for a VC in the first meeting is to understand as much about the business, market and team as possible.

How do the founders know each other? How do they interact with each other? Are they passionate? How qualified are they? What would it be like to work with them?

Concerning business, it is very common the entrepreneur will be asked to walk through the "business model generation framework", also known as "business model canvas": value proposition, key activities, key partners, major assets, channels of distribution, customer segments, cost structure and revenue streams. Is the problem worth solving and if the startup succeeds, how valuable would it be?

Can the company articulate its value proposition simply? Can the team explain how it will go to market? Do they have a good understanding of the competition? How concentrated is the market? What kinds of moves are the incumbents making and how they change the market? How might the startup disrupt this market? It is important to consider the VC will do a market size validation after the meeting. The first thing he will do is to verify whether market size matches the data the company has presented.

Other questions in the first interview will be related to what secret or insight the founding team have made that the rest of the market has not yet realized, and what discontinuity in the market they can leverage to win large share.

6.3. Validation

After the first meeting, the investor will do some homework, related to check whether the statements presented are true and to research a bit more about the team. He will probably look up the founders on LinkedIn, send a few emails for references and then wait to hear back on some initial reference calls.

6.4. Communication

As previously seen, it is crucial the entrepreneur team makes sure the whole team is up to date on the plan. That might start with the CEO giving the investor pitch to the whole organization and distributing the current business plan document to everyone. Make sure all business processes are documented and integrated, to avoid misunderstandings. If everyone gives a different story, you have no story.

Then take time to review and resolve any personnel distractions. You need to brief the investor early if there are pending changes that have to be made or conflicts that may become apparent during the due diligence process. Ask everyone to update their resume and profiles in social media, and personally call probable references, so there are no surprises.

To avoid panic, don't let the due diligence process be a surprise to the team. Communicate what is happening and why to everyone. Make yourself available to answer any questions, show your enthusiasm and explain both the positives and negatives of the external investment process.

You should use this opportunity to validate satisfaction and support from your reference customers, partners and vendors. If you find open issues that can't be immediately resolved, be sure to proactively communicate these to the investors with an action plan, rather than hope they won't be found.

Anyway, you must keep in mind a strong recommendation about sharing information and providing reference customers with the investor: never share customer names or details until the investment agreement is closed. You should assume the investor will go away anytime and you won't want your main customers know you were to sell your company but you couldn't because there is no interest in the market! Additionally, it is not recommended the investor speak with them until you are a single company with a single strategy, roadmap and message to your customers.

6.5. Due diligence process start

The formal due diligence process begins at this point and there will be some more meetings before the investor makes a decision. Follow up meetings are typically dedicated to metrics and the future of the company.

There will be a high focus on pipeline. How many customers or users are there? How often are they using it? What are CAQ, LTV and churn metrics? How do those compare with industry benchmarks?

Regarding the product roadmap, the investor will probably require the entrepreneur team provide a good sense of where the company is going and why. As a consequence, it is probable some forecast will have to be put on the table.

Some questions about the financing plan will arise in these meetings: what are the major buckets of expenditures? How do they change over time? Is the revenue plan reasonable? What are the key metrics for the business?

It is possible the investor will ask for some experts in the industry, who can help him better understand the dynamics in the sector. It is also possible he will invite them to meet the entrepreneur team as well.

In case there are other investors in the company, the VC or business angel will want a final meeting with all of them, in order to discuss further details and dig a bit more about the march of the company.

6.6. Key personnel review

In all cases an investor will ask to talk to all key players and will likely follow up by calling references and prior associates to verify background, commitment and experience. Since investors tend to invest in people rather than the idea, the personnel review is normally the highest priority part.

6.7. Term sheet

The investor will want to sign the term sheet at this point. It is the moment the lawyers step in and it is the right time to perform the legal due diligence. At this stage, details like how well-formed the company is are important, as well as whether there are skeletons in the closet, like fired co-founders, large debts, consultants who are owed shares or pending lawsuits.

The investor will challenge an arm wrestle with the entrepreneur –figuratively speaking– to see how a founder negotiates.

After that, the term sheet will be probably signed and few more discussion may continue before the money is in the company bank account. The game is on!

7. Be prepared for many questions

If you are raising money for your company and you want to pitch to angel investors or venture capitalists, then there are a few important things to know that savvy investors care about.

Despite an entrepreneur may be expecting to be asked about his team, market segments, financial projections, go-to-market strategy or exit strategy, you may face some sort of unexpected questions, like the ones presented in this section.

Far from watching out investors asking the questions below, as you will read in chapter 8, it is important to note the investors who ask the following questions are the ones that care about your business and will accompany you well until the end of your venture together.

You may never get asked these questions, or maybe not as directly as they are asked here, but you should be prepared and have answers to them.

Who believes in you and how can I get in touch with him?

What the investor is looking for here is who are your mentors and advisers. He likes to know that there are people who believe in you, your ideas, your potential, and abilities.

What entrepreneurs do you admire and why?

This is a fun question. Even if you are not asked this question, work it into your pitch because you can tell a lot about people by who they admire.

In this case, keep in mind the importance in the answer to this question is more in why you admire someone than the relevance of the person you admire.

How do you track trends in your market?

Investors want to know that you are aware of your industry, as well as where you go to find data to stay on top of industry trends. Things change very quickly today, particularly if you are in the technology business, so be prepared to share how you find data about your customers and industry, as well as how you apply those findings to your business.

It is important you have trusted sources of information. For example, it is better if you mention IDC, Forrester or Gartner reports about technology trends than a blog or a press release.

Can you tell me a story about a customer using your product?

This should automatically be included in your pitch presentation anyway. The best pitches are the ones that open with a story about how your product or service is helping your customer. Use real names and be as specific as possible about the "pain" that customer had before he used your product and how you have alleviated or addressed that pain. At the end of any presentation, it is the stories the audience will remember, so be sure to craft an excellent customer story.

How do you know how much money you need? Could you scale your business with less?

All investors want to know how much money you need to scale your business, but you had better know what you are going to spend it on and whether you could scale your business with less money. If you could scale, how much less funding and what would you be sacrificing as a result? It is actually a very good idea to have multiple budgets and financial forecasts developed in your business plan so that you can address three different growth models for scaling your business, depending on the amount of money invested in your venture.

How can I connect with five of your current customers?

Only if an investor finds your pitch interesting he will want to begin the due diligence process. During due diligence he will ask a lot about your customers: who they are, how you know who they are, how you find them, what they think of your product, how they are using it, whether that matches your usage intentions, how you interact with them, etc.

What will your market look like in five years as a result of using your product or service?

This is another opportunity to tell the growth of your company through sharing a compelling story. Paint the picture of your customers' future as a result of using your product or service for five years. This helps show the investors that you are able to envision and think critically about how your product and your customer will evolve over time.

What mistakes have you made thus far in this business and what have you learned?

Investors expect business leaders to experience failure. Failure is part of the equation of growth and it is where all of the great learnings come from.

I once had an investor say to an entrepreneur: "I look forward to talking with you again in three months after you have secured those *beachhead* customers, because I know you are going to make mistakes and learn from them. So call me again when you have experienced those mistakes". That was such a powerful statement to hear from a highly respected investor. It is not just that he was giving the entrepreneur permission to fail, but he was giving him the confidence to get out there and call the companies he wanted to do business with. Many said no, but the entrepreneur moved on to the next and kept going until he founded one that agreed. Then the real learning began and it was those gems that he reported back to the investor. He was impressed by his perseverance, his confidence and his ability to communicate his company's value proposition in such a passionate way.

What if three years I think you are not the right person to continue running this company?

Often times —particularly with high-growth startups— the founding CEO does not remain the CEO who scales the company beyond the startup phase and investors ask this question to make sure you don't have "founderitis", that is, when a founder's ego gets in the way of the company growth and the founder refuses or makes it hard to step down or out of the position he holds. It is really good to know what type of entrepreneur you are, as this will make it that much easier to know what you don't know. This is another thing investors want to know you know. Knowing these categories gives you a vocabulary to discuss your strengths and your limitations.

It is important to have people on your team with a combination of the following strengths and abilities. It is also equally important for you to know where you fit into the mix, know what you don't know and be prepared to exit gracefully when the time comes —because it inevitably will:

- **The idea generator**: you are the visionary, you come up with the great next big idea, your thoughts are not limited by what you hear from your peers, the media, the market, etc.

- **The innovator**: you can write code, build things, sew things, invent things, and create something for others to sell. Innovators are typically not the same people who sell what they create.

- **The starter**: you are great at creating a team from nothing and launching a new product or service. You know what it takes to write a solid business plan, implement and track that plan, research and respond to market trends, and surround yourself with people who are smarter than you.

- **The changer**: you are not only great at being a change agent, but you thrive from doing it. These people make the best "turn-around CEOs" – those who enter an existing company, access the situation, recruit change ambassadors, create a new bold plan, make tough decisions (close a business, fire people, hire people, discontinue a product, etc.) and re-position a company for optimal growth –and even sometimes dissolution.

- **The grower**: you are someone who loves "a diamond in the rough". You see the potential in people, products and markets, and know whether they are worth investing time, money and energy into improving. You typically don't like starting new things. Instead, you prefer to take something good that someone else has started and turn it into something great. A talent desperately needed in most companies. This person can take a company from surviving to thriving.

- **The exiter**: you are someone who knows what it takes to position a company or person for exit. That exit is usually merging with another company, acquiring other companies or taking a company public. This is a rare skill set and these people are typically not the starters.

It is important you assess yourself, and ask for your peers to assess you, to get a full picture of how much of each kind of entrepreneur are you and thus hire a team that fulfills those roles where you are not strong.

Have you ever been fired from a job? Tell me about it

This is one of those questions that makes people feel uncomfortable, but that is not the intention of asking it. Rather, it is to see how you respond to a challenging question, as well as learn more about some challenges you have experienced in previous jobs and how you communicate those challenges.

I had one investor tell me that he only invests in entrepreneurs who have been fired from previous jobs. His rationale was that it showed him you were most likely someone who challenged the status quo and ruffled feathers. Although that is not the case for everyone who has gotten fired, it does allow for a conversation about the type of employee you were for others and some potential mistakes you may have made earlier in your career, as well as what you learned from those experiences.

At the end of the day investors want to invest in leaders who are movers, shakers, creators and have the ability to inspire others.

BENJAMIN C. LAWSON

8. Beware the fake investors

I want to add a chapter to highlight some circumstances an entrepreneur may face when considering external investment. Sometimes, one hears of horror stories about investors. Many are misunderstandings while others are just false, but some are sadly true.

There are some individuals who may claim investors themselves but whose real intentions are to steal intellectual property, business models or simply overload a competitor with due diligence related work to get a time advantage for their companies. It is important an entrepreneur identifies such *fake* investors, in order to choose the right financing venture for his company and avoid a waste of valuable time.

Financial institutions are bound by a regulation called KYC (Know Your Customer). It is time we created KYI for investors. You should know who is investing, why he is investing, who he is, how he made his money, what else he is up to, what he is like to work with, what is his temperament and risk appetite, etc.

Before anything, I recommend you do some digging on the people you are going to target: creep on their profiles in AngelList (www.angel.co), CrunchBase (www.crunchbase.com), LinkedIn (www.linkedin.com) and other sites. Check to see if they blog, tweet, judge at

Startup Weekends, mentor at accelerators, speak at conferences or do things that the vast majority of other investors do. Are they talking about their existing investments? Do they add value to industry conversations? Do they seem credible? Do they appear mostly sane?

There are nine red flags you should consider to stop dealing with a supposed investor:

8.1. Red flag 1: no online profile

If they don't have an online profile of any description, be a little wary. There are some super-wealthy people who obviously don't want to be on LinkedIn, Facebook, Twitter and such platforms. But in general terms, someone who has zero online profile should be put into quarantine.

8.2. Red flag 2: the man in the middle

If you are constantly dealing through an intermediary, be wary. When you get into Series A/B/C, it is more natural for this to happen. This is what venture capital is, to a certain extent. In angel rounds, if you are not regularly dealing directly with the angel, this is likely a pattern that will repeat. Also, you run the risk of Chinese whispers and subsequent misunderstandings.

Added to that, if someone is thinking of giving you anything between $5,000 and $500,000, he should probably want to look at you in the eye and talk face to face. Likewise, if you're giving someone a significant share of your company, you should want to spend time with him. If you ask to meet an investor and that never happens for various spurious reasons, don't take his money.

8.3. Red flag 3: ask for references

Ask to talk to companies that the investor has previously put money into. If he refuses this or are sketchy about it, then you should be very, very wary. Talking to companies that your investor has previously put money into is pretty normal due diligence for a startup. You should be asking what the investor is like to work with; is he pushy, obnoxious, needy, anxious, cool, useful or just good, bad or indifferent to work with.

The right investors should be happy to share this info with you. The bad ones won't want you to find out that information. Anyway, you don't need the investor's permission to perform this research. If he has investments listed on LinkedIn, AngelList or other places, just connect directly with the founder or CEO and ask him.

8.4. Red flag 4: valuation expertise

Watch out for nonsense valuations. The less sophisticated the investor, the more of your company he will want. The classic instance is where the investor wants 51% of your business. In most funding rounds you should be aiming to give away between 10% and 25% of your company. The lower end implies you are a hot deal or you are doing something really well. The higher end implies it is riskier or perhaps the traction is not that great. In early rounds, a rule of thumb is that anything above 25% is too high and can create a disincentive for founders and staff.

More important, it can expel future investors in next rounds.

8.5. Red flag 5: "strange" term sheets

Watch out for people who are not at least reasonably amenable to standardized term sheets. Seedsummit (www.seedsummit.org) and many others have produced great templates that are pretty standard. Watch out for things like participating liquidity preferences (1x liquidity preference is probably right, others would argue it is pretty standard). Watch out for warrants, vesting clauses that are overly punitive, full-ratchet anti-dilution clauses and things like that. If you don't understand these terms, you need to. At this point you need to get a lawyer, and not any lawyer but a good one in startups.

8.6. Red flag 6: knowledge and contact network

Watch out for people who only bring cash to the table. Introductions, advice, connections and guidance are the most useful things that early-stage companies can get. The right type of angel —usually one who has been there and done that before— is worth 10x their investment in this regard. He will shill for you at conferences, introduce you to people, act as an additional BD/sales/HR person and generally add way more than just cash to the equation. Don't ask what you can do for your investors but what they can do for you.

Be upfront about asking what else he is bringing

outside of cash. Can he introduce you to potential clients or useful contacts? Can he help in hiring or international growth? Does he know the reporter covering your area at the biggest trade publication or at the FT? Can he connect you with bigger investors when the time is right?

8.7. Red flag 7: unrealistic expectations

Watch out for people who want overly complex financial projections when you are pre-revenue or pre-product. Anyone with a brain in his head knows it is guesswork and a waste of time.

Smart early-stage investors back the team, the market and the idea —probably in that order. If someone is emphasizing his most interest in the results for five-year projections, you should think he is not an experienced investor or even he is trying you to waste your time with him instead of doing things to grow your business or find the right investor. As a rule of thumb, never waste too much time on projections.

8.8. Red flag 8: most people don't say "no"

Watch out for people who drop off the face of the planet after giving you a soft commitment. As a species, we are not great at saying "no" to people, so a lot of investors will simply break off contact instead of saying "no" explicitly. If someone drops off the radar after saying he is in, it probably means he is out. Otherwise, in case he is going on holiday, having surgery or something else that prevents him from replying to an email or WhatsApp, he will probably tell you.

8.9. Red flag 9: gut feeling

If your gut feeling is bad about someone the first time you meet him, pay attention to that. You don't have to be best mate with all your investors —in fact, you shouldn't be. But you do have to at least tolerate them. If you are lucky, you will be talking to and emailing them once a month for the next five to ten years. Gut feeling is important.

Gut feeling is not to discount an investment straight away but if someone feels off, creepy or just not right, spend a bit more time figuring out why, and definitely do at least one more meeting to double check that feeling.

8.10. Conclusion

This is just a small set of things you should be looking for when you are talking to early-stage or angel investors. It is equally as applicable to later-stage investments but, in the early stages of a business, this has to be taken even more seriously. The people you take on as investors at the start can be a huge predictor of the success of future funding rounds, or even the company as a whole.

Suppose you trust in an investor that, after entering in the company equity, happens to be one of the leading fugitives from a foreign country. As you can probably imagine, having someone like that in your board is going to make a lot less appealing your company for a tier-one VC invest in your next round.

Do your homework. Do it early. Do it often. Don't be afraid to ask for references and more info about the person who is investing. If he is sufficiently motivated and interested in you, he should be probably happy to do it. If he is sufficiently smart, he will respect you asking.

CPSIA information can be obtained
at www.ICGtesting.com
Printed in the USA
LVOW11s2130150118
563010LV00001B/38/P